Ephphatha
"Be Opened"

Matt Wall

This book is dedicated
With love to

My wife,
Donna;

My seven sons and four daughters,
Matt, Mark, Patricia, Mike, Laura, Mary,
Walter, Daniel, Katie, Jon, and George;

Arnold Plank, the Superintendent of
Torrance Unified School District;

And to the high school students who inspired
Me from West High School in Torrance and
Ventura High School

Contents

Preface xi
The Interface xiii
   Chapter I 1
   1. The Source 1
   2. Lovable 1
   3. Place 2
   4. Moments 2
   5. Fear Is the Lock 3
   6. The Pace 3
   7. Alive 4
   8. Solution 4
   9. Spark 5
   10. Windows 5
   11. Things 6
   12. Mirrors 6
   13. Comparison 7
   14. The Sides of Truth 8
   15. Jacaranda 8
Chapter II 11
   1. The Deepest Desire 11
   2. The Flow 11
   3. Fragile 12
   4. Ideas 13
   5. Why? 13
   6. Unfolding 14
   7. Change, See Reality 15
   8. Children 16
   9. Communicate Now 16
   10. People 16

11. Taped	18
12. Dear Woman	21
13. Friendship	22
Chapter III—Beauty	**23**
1. Beautiful	23
2. Communicate	23
3. True Measure	24
4. Presents	25
5. Person Value	26
6. Love	27
7. Lights	28
8. The Stars	29
9. Dying	29
10. Cinderella	30
Chapter IV—Truth	**31**
1. Truth	31
2. Said	31
3. Love and Birth	31
4. Anger	32
5. On Being Present	32
6. Treasure Hunt	33
7. Value Is in the Opposite	33
8. Conversion	34
9. Home	34
10. Some Words	34
11. Inside	35
12. Morning Thoughts	36
Chapter V—Life	**37**
1. Yours	37
2. He Walks Along	37
3. Trees	37

- 4. The Rose 38
- 5. Luck 38
- 6. Fear 38
- 7. Flowers 39
- 8. Masses 39
- 9. Fall 39
- 10. Living 40
- 11. Moments 41
- 12. Trip 42
- 14. The Choice 42
- 15. The Castle 43
- 16. Face to Face 43
- 17. Gifts 44
- 18. Seamless 44
- 19. On Growing 45

Chapter VI—Seeds 47
- 1. Man Is Responsible 47
- 2. The Farmer 47
- 3. Seeds 47
- 4. Flowers 48
- 5. Harvest 48
- 6. He Grows 49
- 7. She Grows 49
- 8. Marriage 50

Chapter VII—Stories 51
- 1. Tables 51
- 2. The City 51
- 3. High School 52
- 4. Broken Hearts 54
- 5. Convert 54
- 6. The Search 55

- 7. Inside Outside 56
- 8. You 56
- 9. Choose 56
- 10. Wasted 57
- 11. Waste 57
- 12. Dump 58
- 13. Captain 58
- 14. Toy 58
- 15. Danger 59
- 16. Dream 59
- 17. Playmate 60
- 18. Little Kids 60
- 19. Off to Work 60

Chapter VIII—Teacher 63
- 1. Teacher 63
- 2. Teach 63
- 3. The World 63
- 4. Lifetimes 64
- 5. Love and Growing 64
- 6. Stop Now, Step Back 65
- 7. Today 66
- 8. Age 67
- 9. Peace 67
- 10. Patient 68
- 11. Waiting 68
- 12. Unreal 69
- 13. Hey 69
- 14. Some Facts of Life 70
- 15. Two Choices Only 72
- 16. Reality 72
- 17. Lamp Oil 74

18. Modern Man 75
  19. Today... 76
Chapter IX—Mary 79
  1. Family 79
  2. Mother 79
  3. Mary 79
  4. Hope 80
  5. Habits 80
  6. Tapes 81
Chapter X—God 83
  1. Ineffable 83
  2. Treasures... 83
  3. Call.. 83
  4. Love Yourself 85
  5. Desire to Love 86
  6. Special 87
  7. Today's Life 87
  8. To Grow 88
  10. To Love Anyone.. 89
  11. Love Is One 90
  12. Lord 90
  13. Life and Death 90
  14. Grace 92
  15. More... 92
  16. The Presence 93
  17. Man's Highest Activity 93
  18. The Heart 94
  19. On Being—On Going 94
  20. Together.. 95
  21. Now is the Time 96
  22. Civilization 97

23. Follow	99
24. His Plan	99
25. Seasoning	100
26. The Passageway	100
27. Se man Tics	100

Preface

Dear Ones,
It's time to say things, these ideas that are in us all.
These dreams are so alive in some of us.
They flow through us like a stream, like the value of true love . . . the wonder of it and the fact of our sameness and uniqueness which melts in love and becomes a oneness.
Matthew J. Wall

The Interface

What a time to be alive! The other night, Jon, my son, looked up at the moon. As I wondered at its beauty, Jon asked, "Did a man really stand on that moon?"
We race off always to another and another and yet another place, never satisfied, always hurrying. While what we most need is to be quiet inside. We search and search for meaning and it is carved in each of our hearts. We play music and hear words that tell us absolute truths, and we pull the plug and go on in our deafness.
There is no time; there is no place. There is only the interface. He stands there for us always with abundant love, waiting for us to turn our face.

Chapter I

1. The Source

We cannot become discouraged because the father of mankind is still there. He is still standing facing us and waiting. This interface God and man face to face will always be there. We can see Him in so many ways. In the changing colors of the leaves, in the wind and waves, in the rocks, and in the waters of the lakes and streams and oceans, all of His home for us. Most important though, we can see Him in the people that are in each moment of our lives. His light shines from caring eyes. I must listen to each person and really be for each person all that I can be. I must search through all the words and gestures and actions and know that God sent just this one to me now. This moment He stands before me maybe hidden away for the most part in this person who is with me now. Let me be aware and alive to His presence.

2. Lovable

Where is this interface, the being face to face with God? Where is this place where spirits meet and melt into a reality of love - yes, into a person who is living love? Each person is! And what is, is. Each person is 100 percent lovable just as they are. Like a flower in bud holds the promise of bloom and is perfect in each stage, so a person is now. Follow the example of the flower; it holds its face up to God.

What keeps us from seeing the beauty of each person is the garbage we carry around. What we fail to see is that this garbage, this fear, is in us. We fail to see the loveableness of the other person because of our garbage, not because the other person is not lovable. God loves each of us 100 percent, just as we are. He surrounds us, waiting and hoping that somehow we will see Him in the symbols of His love.

3. Place

The cares and distractions of the world are constantly pulling at us. We seek always a quiet place, a place to be, and loneliness hides away in the quiet. To find God, we have to go alone to the mountain and shut out the rest of the world, and we have to look and see Him in all people, in every person, seen and unseen. We have to see Him in the teeming masses and love them each and all. So we must dare to be a lover in a world that does not know how to love. We must understand that only a few will be able to stand with us for long and know that we cannot stand alone except that God Himself has us in the palm of His hand. WE MUST BE ALIVE!!! We are always face to face with God. His love knows no place.

4. Moments

As we live along, aware of being love in a world needing love, each moment becomes extremely important. As we love in each moment, fear falls away and its lock on us opens so that we are free to be a lover in the next and the next moment. So our life unfolds in moments that become adventures and we begin to see. We notice the color of the eyes, the softness of smiles, and the kindness of hugs.

It is not easy to live in the moments. Cares and distractions are constantly pulling at us. It's almost like trying to keep aware of breathing.

5. Fear Is the Lock

Where are you in each little moment of your life? Are the windows and doors open? Are the paths smooth? Do you know the feelings that come through the door of your open heart?

Each breath is a anew life. Don't look back. The payments due will come up to you as you live. Be in each moment all you can be. See clearly the good.

Fear is the lock on the doors and windows of your heart. Fear locks you in and others out. Fear kills creativity. Fear eliminates freedom. Embarrassment is fear. Control is the child of fear. Fear freezes trust.

How do we fight fear? Dare to love in each moment. Decide to love in each moment.

6. The Pace

We must slow down; we must dare to take our time and listen, really listen, to others. Only in our acceptance can they hope to grow, to become at peace, to understand, and to get free of the prisons of things and ideas. So we keep our eyes on Him. All we have is the interface. There is not time, there is no place. He said, "I will restore all things. I will make all things new." Oh, man, see Him love you in the beauty of His creation, it is all for you. The second lifetime lasts forever. So, let God set your pace; always keep in mind the interface.

7. Alive

We can only really be in the moments. GOD IS NOW! In this moment when we walk out the door. In the realization that all men and women are in love with each other in the finest, purest way. Fear keeps us from being and singing out their love. In each moment we have the choice to be or not to be.

Life cannot be lived one whole day at a time. We cannot really be if we are not alive to all each moment holds. All the light color and adventure.

Jess Lairds' book, *I Ain't Much Baby, But I'm All I've Got*, says to take living five minutes at a time. A moment at a time to keep awareness at a high level and acceptance at a peak.

The interface, man and God face to face, can only take place in a moment and a moment. A moment for God is now.

8. Solution

Time holds the solution. The green leaves that give shade, beauty, and privacy to the new fruit are meant to wither, fall, and blend with the seeds, again becoming part of the whole - growing, becoming, passing and changing, in the time that holds the solution that becomes the wine, giving joy to the living.

9. Spark

When you first see another person, one you have never seen before, I mean really look and see them with your heart and mind right, then that first look is like a spark. Most important is the spark and whether it is there or not.

We are meant to have a spark for each look, each encounter, each person. To do this, we must be consistently and constantly conscious and present - really be ourselves, asserting that self, so that others know us, really know us.

10. Windows

We go to the windows of Heaven and what do we find? They are pasted over with slogans and ads, cars and trucks are keeping us from seeing in, or nudes are pinned across the glass like faces.

We go to the windows of Heaven and what do we see? The dust and dirt of the world keep us from seeing in.

We go to the windows of Heaven, and what do we do? We refuse to look except for an occasional glance because of our fear and because, as we look, we see a mirror view of us, our real selves.

Oh where are these windows of Heaven? Oh, - yes, they are the eyes of those who surround us every day.

11. Things

Things can never make you happy. The giving away of things can. Alone you can never be happy. Unless you are conscious of the presence of another person you are dead. If I was not conscious of the presence of you, why should I write these words, and, who am I without you to look at me and be my friend.

The hills in the desert "become" because some men see in them stark beauty. Yes Lord, you are in these hills. You are the life in them and even more. Somehow you know we need them standing there with no trees just sand and dust, rocks and shrubs, "alone."...I am called to them. I see their purity. I see what they have given up. I see that without things on them they have freedom and stark beauty. Rains come and only make them glisten. The hot sun can pour down and they do not melt and shrink. And Lord, in the moonlight, they seem strong like arms surrounding us, protecting us. Thank you Lord for lessons of the desert.

12. Mirrors

We see in the eyes of others far more and more as we begin to love and to grow in love:

Lovely eyes—mirrors into the chamber where love lies.

Lovely eyes—that somehow know that time is the key to eternity.

Lovely eyes—and moments tip the tumblers that would open the lock.

Lovely eyes—of peace and hope.

Lovely eyes—open, that show me you in your wonderful beauty.

Lovely eyes—whose light shines from smiles and covers the pain in me.

Lovely eyes—bright and sweet and filled with promise.

Lovely eyes—sad and filled with tears of grief.

Lovely eyes—filled with the joy of knowing the unlimited love of God.

Lovely eyes—drawing in the creation like the ocean draws the streams of the world.

13. Comparison

EARTH—In the center of the earth, it's all fire and heat and molten rock. Then, out away from the center, there are areas of hardness, areas of softness and saturation. Through all these, the rivers of rock and fluid seem to flow, while on the surface, we have the deserts, oceans, lakes and streams, rivers, trees, grasses, snow-capped mountains and fertile valleys.

HEART—In the center of the heart, it is all fire and heat and molten love. Then, out farther there are areas of hardness and areas of softness, tears, and laughter. Through all these, like rivers of openness and barriers of coldness, runs the fluid of tears and the hardness of fears, while, on the surface, we have dry times and happy times, pools of joy, caverns of sorrow, soft times, quiet times, and we open to love times.

We compare God's creation with our hearts. We look for places where we can meet God: mountain tops, way out to sea, in the desert where the silence leaves us standing and hearing…He is always within, standing face to face.

14. The Sides of Truth

Truth has two sides, two faces, an inner face and an outer face. Mathematic truth, electricity, magnetism, gravity and stars. Also, the mysterious goodness of true love, the flame of truth. So, we can see it and we can feel it.

When we follow truth and are open to it in our lives, it causes us to dive deep and become in tune with the fullness, the immensity, the eternal unlimitedness of our God. There are more stars in the Milky Way than grains of sand on the earth. There are more galaxies in the universe than stars in the Milky Way. There is a place for us, a place uniquely set aside for each of us. It is complete and full and special. The search continues…

15. Jacaranda

The seeds, set in the base of the flower like in an amphitheater, closed then slowly opening to the sunrises and the sunsets of life. Time passing color of the petals slowly coming on. The seeds close waiting through darkness of the closed bud and then into the first light coming through the petals. Each of us like a seed in the arena. Then, as we go along we watch the drying up and the falling out. The shriveling of the beauty in the petals and we too in our turn fall into the mud of the world.

Knowing in our hearts that there is a better place but having to go this route to get there. Days pass and feet trample us into the mud and the mire of the soil and then if we do not lose heart we are born again new, increasing and growing up and up seeing in our heart the flower that someday will be at the top of the tree.

Chapter II

1. The Deepest Desire

Intimately, the wind caresses the trees, the leaves thrill to the touch. With roots deep and limbs outstretched, the tree reaches up, full of faith, hope and joy. In all seasons the tree stands tall and reaches out and up. Time passes and its seeds are placed in the ground by the wind that loves it. The sun and water renew it. It is surrounded by life; it has continued. The wind favors its little ones and when the tree dies, its spirit lingers on. The body it used rots away and becomes food for the little ones. The cycle continues. Man, it is the same for you, your spirit lingers on waiting.

2. The Flow

In all creation, in each minute thing, there is a flow. Lines, curves, and circles of the flow are etched, as in the grains of wood and as the swirls of current in the pond. These are reminders of universes upon universes. They are reminders of the infiniteness of our God. We are in the flow, moving in all ways, inside and outside—wholly moving—the lines of our movement etch themselves in our faces as we pass along. Make our lines lines of trust, lines of joy, lines of caring.

Love is the openness of pure, sweet friendship. Like a river, life passes us—through, in and with—and we cannot leave this eternal river. The trail goes on and on and on, yet when we look back, we only see the vague pathway. We must go on to search for the answer.

And the answer, add one hundred years to now. What matters? Did we love? Were we a true friend?

3. Fragile

The earth is fragile. Its natural systems are tough and smooth and are ongoing, able to overcome natural things; but, when the natural is perverted it throws the whole body off. It kicks and shakes the foundation. It weakens the structure and that's what man is doing in many ways today. Man holds onto desires and fabricates needs by making gods out of things and by wanting more and more and more of these things. The earth is fragile, but the creator knows man. In everything the creator made He put renewal and restoration. Time will turn the rotten into food for flowers. The things of man soon fall away to rust and rot as the creator tends His creation. Time will bring back all the beauty that ever was and more and more and more to infinity.

We must work along with the creator and realize these things He made and gave to us are gifts to us, meant for our good and for our study.

The only thing that gives value to anything is people's faith. Anything can become an idol. The only value is faith and faith belongs to God alone. It is God sharing Himself with man, drawing man to a oneness with truth and love.

4. Ideas

It's funny about ideas. They come to individuals separately. Many times the greatest ones come to a person all alone and quiet. Even stranger is the way they come like thin cobwebs of spun gold, at first easily brushed off. To really be aware and catch onto and hold these golden thoughts, a person has to be eating good food and being physically sound, having exercised so that the body is functioning with maximum proficiency – a person with a sound, caring mental state, undrugged by television, junk food, depressants, and/or stimulants, just eating good food and drinking water. A person also has to be free of fear to a great extent. Guilt and fear cut deep into consciousness.

For your physical sickness be glad. For your pain and cut and ache be glad. For your mental anguish be ashamed. For God's love overcomes this also. For the immorality of yourself start now to be true in your friendships and to practice self-control. Get into really caring for others. For the immorality of yourself and others say prayers and live in moments listening and seeing clearly.

5. Why?

Why are you and I alive? Because, like Pinocchio, we were made to return the love freely, the love that we received from our loving maker. Pinocchio went out into the world of cats and foxes, ignored real love, and made an ass out of himself. He was, like us, meant to love his maker. How do we love our maker? By really being ourselves for His honor. The mind will do whatever the self commands, for the mind is the servant of self. The mind will work in all possible ways to support whatever the self thinks it is. If the self honors his maker, the mind in him will strive to bring about constant honor of God.

You and I will be in love forever, exploring the depth beyond the universe forever more and more. Life is the passageway to the center of light. Education is enlightenment.

Sincerity means without wax… Did you ever consider the size of an apple or an orange, a cherry or a pineapple? Every moment is an adventure. Every person is special. Every idea is alive. Love is the opening of hearts. It cannot be seen or explained because love is not a physical thing.

To forgive, to cleanse, to purge, to cut off all the foulness, to take away the odor, the stench, and allow the healing to take place. Time passes. The plastic surgeon who is Jesus will change the patterns and weave and restore so that the scar is gone, and the smooth flow of love will be seen in the lines of the skin. In the eyes will be seen joy, hope and love. To make new to restore with love, by love and for love. Pure, real, love.

6. Unfolding

When it's a time for nothingness and loneliness crowds in to fill your heart. All seems so hopeless and empty—nothing—nothing can fill this time unless we look inside to really find ourselves and know that it's all good. It's unfolding like a rose. In time the spring will come never to leave.

7. Change, See Reality

      Oh how much I want to change you. Oh how much I see in you. Yes, I see through all the stains and bottles and smoke. I see a different real you. Locked in a prison I see a powerful, kind and tender person. I see a person who cares for children and flowers and soft songs. Why can't you too see the reality of you? I know now that I can't change you. All I can do is go on loving and hoping and living through the abuse of your unreality...I love you.

      Step back from the scenes you are in. Take time to float there above those scenes and to realize that many times those places are not where the real you wants to be. Look also and see the changes you need to make so that you can know your own goodness. For you are destined to be good. Yes? Your deepest desire is to be good. The decision is yours alone. Say a prayer for help. Call out for renewal and restoration. The love of God is unlimited and eternal. The greatest tasks are based in simplicity. The greatest desires are based in the deepest innermost recesses of our hearts. The greatest good comes from the other side of the mirror. We must reflect. We must be like a purified diamond, to create from within a good world and all that's in it.

8. Children

Children bring love and happiness! True? Yes! True, but love and happiness are not what we sometimes think. The alternative—no children—brings things and clothes and bank accounts. If this was it! If there was not something more. Then why have children? But what could God value more than children. From children love can flow.

9. Communicate Now

Hey family let's communicate! How? Let's talk about how we feel. How? Let's take away the barriers that keep us apart. How? Let's be alive for at least tonight, alive to each other. How? To start—throw out your television set...

10. People

In friendship is the soil of growing and the fuel and the fruit and the very reason for existence, because God is the unity that it leads to.

Look for the best things about the people who surround you and tell them of their individual beauty. Tell it with smiles and touch and words too. But be careful of words. He who judges, he who does not accept others as is, no matter what the reason, is dead and buried. God is the judge.

Time passes fast, elementary school, middle school, high school. We learn a little here and there about things, people, and ideas. We dream a lot in the first grades. Things become very important in the seventh, eighth, and ninth grades. People become very important in the tenth, eleventh, and twelfth grades. Then high school ends and the flow of people changes as their business increases. The flow shrinks to only a few and it's a drag sometimes.

Things can make people happy for short times and so we try more things and different people but still it's no good. What goes wrong?

The dreams of the very young about people, things, and ideas are true dreams, and they become the fire of discovery and adventure in high school.

High school is a place to increase person foundation. A place to get into hope. Yes, hope that the dreams you dreamed when very young can and will come true for you, that the friends you had and the friends you now have will be true and good and forever friends, that the idea of being a person liked by everyone is possible, and that kindness will be the final result.

The dreams of this world get lost in a maze of physical desires for things and people and the ideas or dreams fade in a dullness and uncleanness.

Physical love is empty in the long run. It serves its purpose like a thing and was not meant to be idolized. Only in the heart do we really live. But how do we get to this land of the heart? By deciding to be a friend – just a friend to everyone we meet. In school we learn a lot about the body and the mind but the heart is a mysterious part. It's hard to teach about what you cannot see. It's difficult to teach a class in being unique to a whole room of unique students. Besides, it cannot be seen or held in your hand, so how could you grade it? However, nothing has lasting meaning until it is in the heart. To love is the meaning and the destiny of all life. All other things will fall into rot and be replaced. The heart (the love) only will last. Love is not a physical thing. Love is so very simple many people never grasp it even though they search and search and reach and reach.

He sees all—He hears all—He is in us—He is the heart of our hearts, and we are in the heart of His Heart. In the land of the heart the fears that camouflage the gate, the pains and scars that cover its face are matched on the body of him who stands there knocking. When the son of man was lifted up all fear was banished. The son became the light of the world of heartland. Not even death can stand in the light of the son's love. As we live on in His love we are free of all fear. Love is now—in each moment. Everything that happens is interlaced with love for those who live in heartland. It is so very rich only small spoons can be used.

11. Taped

He was unaware of it, but everything he heard was taped and every movement was recorded. When he opened his eyes it was videotaped with sound and the vibrations were not left out. When he talked all his words were powerful messages in the tapes. After a time, a more sensitive system became operable and recorded the complete detailed specific elements of every scene – not only sound and movement, but all sensations and vibrations of touch and feel. All was stored in memory in perfect order. All input was considered true and good.

This procedure continued and as time passed a program was formed from the data by the self (an innocent beautiful creature full of good). This program was reinforced constantly and it included if statements and other decision points as well. In every case the decisions were based on stored data and they reinforced the program pattern. This program created relationships, selected associates, and planned entertainment, and all the plans, relationships, and associations fit the pattern. The self was unaware the computer was in control. The mind influenced the self through tapes from the past much like the kings of old were influenced by their advisors, only much more so.

Finally, through some circumstance, some crazy scene or relationship, some opposite situation, grace entered and the self awoke and found that he was in a sealed room. As he looked around he saw a computer with a video screen. A tremendous storage unit, and the room had a dusty corner way away from the computer where a door could be vaguely seen in the dust. The computer was perfectly shiny and clean except for the storage unit which even though it was sealed had an odor to it. Along one wall were shelves lined with rows of disks and cassette tapes.

He sat in the chair. It seemed somehow familiar, but all the vagueness washed away and clearness filled him. In his awakened state he saw clearly that he was the operator. He had been playing tapes unaware really, unconscious. In the days that followed he played tapes. For the first time he really saw that some were bad and some were good, at least they seemed good. The good became clearer to him as he became more awake. He knew that he wanted this place he was in to be a place of caring and kindness, a safe place. Days...weeks passed.

He changed some tapes, deleting things and adding things like: To be clean is good. To be aware of others is good. To concentrate is good. To be in the now is good. When he looked into his video screen and moved his capsule-like room around, the others he saw seemed special, and he noticed the sky. He saw the trees and the flowers. It was after that he erased whole sets of disks and tapes. He carefully studied his relationship tapes and his association tapes. He searched out the people he had done wrong to and asked them to forgive him. He forgave in person all those who made him angry or had done him wrong. He changed. He got control of his life. He actually opened the dusty door and went forth "out of his mind;" happy, alive, and into a world of all heart.

The self needs to forever be in the land of heart— only for a time in body and only for a time in mind. Deny self, and set it free of mind and body so that it can go to the oneness of heart, where to listen is to love, perfection is the goal, adventure is the feeling, and Jesus is the pathway.

12. Dear Woman

The beauty of you can be lost in the world. Please consider all the tapes you have and all the reruns. Let me offer to you another thought. In order to grow, a seed must be planted in the dirt and rocks. It must then quietly struggle, break itself open, and climb up through the dark dirt to the surface. At that point where it meets the surface it is fragile, but the source, its roots, in the soil keep sending out strength. Your source is not just your mom or dad or both, it is generations. It is from forever. It is the all of all.

If in your moments you never consider your source, and if you do things to cut it off, damaging the connections with chemical or emotional crisis, eventually you will dry up like a plant without water. No fruit will be able to come from you and no good will enter the world through you.

Dear woman, put aside these momentary thrills that lead to nothingness; for you are a flower of great potential. If you put aside real love for false love you are only hurting yourself. Real love honors the sources, all of them—parents, no matter how they are, teachers, all authority. Above all, real love is true. Real love does not give into thrills. Real love suffers the children to be born and fed and clothed and accepted. Lady, I know what the real you can be like. Please consider. Please rethink where you are, what you are, before it's too late for you to be.

The time is now, for years without flowers make its mark on the beauty of any tree.

(written to a student in Ventura High)

13. Friendship

Friendship is the relationship that exceeds all others. It is the acceptance of another as is. In friendship you cause another to become all that they can be. You cause them to go beyond the barriers that they have set up. The barriers that would keep them locked into a pattern to nowhere. In friendship you never use another, you give to them from the treasure of your heart, you cause them to see inside their own heart to a new place to live, and you bring them to new life. Friends stay young together. Friends stay pure and clean together. Friends are like small children playing together, completely involved in listening to each other and building and creating together. When you feel friendless, no amount of things can fill the void. Remember, you are never friendless, Your friend put those stars in the night sky; your friend made the ocean waves, your friend brings the flowers in the spring, and He crystallizes the trees with winter frost. Your friend...

Chapter III—Beauty

1. Beautiful

You are more beautiful to me than all the stars up in the sky.

You are more beautiful to me than all the rivers, lakes and streams.

You are more beautiful to me than all the trees and flowers and plants.

Because I feel your love for me deep within my heart.

You are more beautiful to me than other people around.

You are more beautiful to me than all the things that man has made.

You are more beautiful to me than ideas and dreams that come to me.

Because I can feel deep within me a mysterious oneness with you.

You are my love forever.

2. Communicate

Communication is personal contact. To listen is to love. To share is to trust. "Say what you know is true in your heart." Real communication is personal contact! We can live in our hearts or in our minds or in our emotions. In real communication a father becomes a father to each person he meets and a mom is a mom to all. We must communicate from the heart and not from other sources so that we are brothers and sisters to each other. Trust is of maximum importance. So, we put aside fear and just be there in our reality, vulnerable. To really communicate, we must put aside fear, living in our hearts and using our body, mind, and emotions as tools, trusting our hearts completely and accepting others as they are. We must say and do only what we know is true in our hearts.

No one is really living who lives in fear. What we admire in actors is their seeming lack of fear. Fear can only be overcome through actual experience. We can experience physically, mentally, and emotionally. These three are separate, equal and one—all at the same time. Fear cannot get to the heart part where life is. Fear is dead. The heart never dies...

3. True Measure

What you look like is never a true measure of the love in your heart. What you have in the way of things is never a true measure of the love in your heart. What you have in the number of friends is never a true measure of the love in your heart. Then what is the true measure of the love in your heart? It is the ability to accept all others as they are with constant hope and unlimited forgiveness, even to death. Because 100 years will surely pass and the only question that has any meaning will surely be asked... Did you love?

So let's look with a new light, the light of acceptance and love. To really be, we must have the ability to stand up and be counted as a lover. We must stand up in love with our enemies, our sick, our foreign, our poor, as well as with our unconcerned friends and joking comrades, who do not see or understand us. We must be lights of love in a dark world even to the death. What is this like? It's like two people setting on a park bench. The step one is to acknowledge each other. The step two is to accept each other as is. The step three is to trust each other with everything in our power. If we get no returning love then we have at least been love in the world.

To live is to love—to love is to live—without love nothing is!!!

4. Presents

The presents, all of them for all time, will never match your presence. Even when you are unsmiling. Even when you are preoccupied. Because, things can never replace people. All things are nothing compared to the poorest, saddest, most diseased, retarded cripple of a person. A person can respond. A person can accept love and caring. A person can give recognition and love back. Be happy that you can give your presence to those around you. Be aware of the gift that you are to others. Be conscious of the goodness of your smile and your kindness. When you accept others as they are, you give them the power to change, to go on living and growing more into being.

5. Person Value

Each person we meet is before us or near us for a reason. Each person who comes flying over us in an airplane or driving by us in a car is there for a reason, not by chance—never by chance. Like the stars are not by chance in the sky, like the sun is not by chance lighting up the world each morning, like the rain, which waters the crops, trees, and flowers, does not come by chance, there is a plan for us in each moment. Only by listening to the quiet voice within can we ever be able to be real in each moment. Only by being alone can we ever hear the quiet voice. Only by overcoming fear will we ever be able to hear and follow the plan for us. The message of the plan is always the same. The how to's are from the quiet voice. The message says be love, be love, be love.

Yes, be love, standing in the field of flowers as the airplane flies over and the old woman looks down out of the plane window. Be love standing there, not knowing that she sees her daughter grown and beautiful in you, her daughter that she aborted years ago. You won't see the tears in her eyes as she silently sits in her airplane seat and disappears into the clouds. Yes, be love sitting at the table early in the morning and the young son comes out to say good morning. He is real standing there. Be real back. Be careful of the mind that says he is taking my silent time. Hug him good morning, and he will hug his son and his son will hug his son and generations of huggers will follow him.

To see clearly it is necessary to get out of self and into seeing others, without comparing or labeling. To be love we must see the acceptableness of each person. If God loves them so must we. Our hope must be like Mary's hope, never ending and full of prayer for them and for ourselves.

6. Love

Love is l-learning o-of v-values e-eternal. The reason for the human heart is to love. In fact, if it does not, it is not.

To be or not to be—not loving is not being. When you really love, nothing is boring. No one is uninteresting. The persons you like are superb pleasure to be with and the persons not easy to like become the greatest gift of all.

In order to have any of this make sense, a person has to get out of his mind and into his heart. The mind cannot figure this out. This love is not a thing of the mind, it's of the heart. In fact, it's not a thing, and has nothing to do with things. Things need to be cleared away so that it's easier for a person to begin to see with heart.

There is a love so great that it holds the stars in the sky; there is a love so great He can bring peace and joy into places that are like graves. There is hope because of Him, hope beyond all reasoning, hope so great that nothing can deter it or mar it.

In time a rose comes forth out of mud, and from it a rose bush and from the rose bush a garden of roses. In time a person grows from out of selfishness and into the light of giving to a place in the hearts of those in need.

To grow is to do the work set before you in the best way you can. In doing this work, you are being a lover. Grades have little meaning. What is important is that you give and do the best effort possible for you. In doing this, in this effort, you will set yourself free from guilt, from the pain of self-doubt; for after all, you have done your best, you have given what you could from your mind and your heart. What more is there for you to give?

The reactions of others are those others' responsibility. If you have loved, what more can you do? If they do not see your love, if they do not honor your personhood, then they have missed the chance to love you back and they, not you, are diminished.

Dare to love in a world of non-lovers. Dare to bring kindness and friendship to a world of fear and hopelessness and you will be planting the first rose in your garden. Remember, the garden is in your heart, the heart must be open or it dies

PEACE   LOVE   JOY

7. Lights

We need to see your lights ahead and other lights behind to know we are not alone. Where do we encounter the interface, the face to face of us and God? In every person, place and thing, God is in His creation. He is the living water within us. Even the rocks cry out, praising Him. To know God you must search in the opposite of the world. To find His riches, seek the world's poor. There is more value in pain than in ice cream sundaes. The mystery of friendship in its truest sense is of the kingdom. The mystery of being able to stand in front of fear and not be afraid even to death because of God's unlimited and eternal love. Fear cannot put out even a small candle of love.

8. The Stars

The space scientist has tools to study the stars, and by the latest observations, he has determined that there are more stars in the Milky Way than there are grains of sand in all the oceans, lakes, rivers and streams of the world. These scientists then go on to mention that there are more galaxies in the universe that there are stars in the Milky Way. The creations of God have no limit. We cannot even dream of the wonders unfolding for each of us. We are made by Him to His image and likeness, and instilled in us is a desire to be like Him—to create.

9. Dying

You are not going to die. No one is. You then have nothing to fear. Go forward doing good and cutting out of your life the things and thoughts that you do not want to take with you. Life is a journey to a special place where everything is always new and clean, where love and kindness are the purpose of lives. Creativity will be the work but work will not be for the fun of it; it will turn it into pure joy. Time and space have no limits. Please understand you can never die. Habits keep you tied down and prevent you from being free.

Repetition in creativity? Never! Every creation is unique. We need each other. Never is a person to be compared to a part or a product. Each is unique and special.

10. Cinderella

Practice love and you cannot even imagine the good that will come to you and everyone around you.

Chapter IV—Truth

1. Truth

The truth comes in simplicity, simple small steps. Little by little the mosaic is created. The immense truth is given in small parts. Like light only a small part can be taken at a time or we are blind. Like sound only a small part can be taken at a time or we are deaf. Like words only a few can be taken at a time or we are confused.

2. Said

What needs to be said is not being said. What needs to be done is not being done. We allow lies to go on and on and fail to stand up and say the truth. We do not do things that need doing. We let the other guy do it and he doesn't. So it never gets done because we fail to assert our reality. We are not conscious of our individual power, beauty, and value.

3. Love and Birth

Love and birth are the only things that have much worth. It seems that all the other sort are there just to give support. If you choose to use and to abuse it's better for you to take a snooze. Man is fulfilled in creativity and relationship. To build up you must clean up. To become you must be. Before he was related he was created.

4. Anger

Most anger is waste. It is burning up energy. Anger is energy spent creating nothing, clearing away nothing. Anger is like burning the rubber on a car. The wheels spin and the car goes nowhere. The tires get wasted.

No one can cause another to be angry, because anger is a decision. The cause of my anger is me. Get beyond the physical, the cause is me. The cause is me in my life. I cause my own anger. I cause my own sadness, I cause my own pain. I cause my own joy. To grow I must be constantly working toward the renewal of me, going over, taping over the old, losing it in the newness of me.

Growing and becoming is a matter of my awareness and acceptance of myself as I am, as I am being loved by God in all ways through the winds and rains of life. Then, I can reach out in awareness and acceptance of others and see the reality of each person I meet. I cannot change them. I can only learn from them what to do and what not to do with my own life. I must say no to those who would bring me to no good. Each person I meet has value, their direction is an example for me as I live my life.

5. On Being Present

How any times have I not been there, maybe more than I have been. Crazy! Being there involves others. Really being there denies self. To be conscious of the other's presence in their words, actions, and thoughts. Consciously being with them in their plans, dreams, hopes, and work without applying possession or jealousy or anything negative. This is a letting of example, your example, shine out in being. Listening is the key element of being there. The less said the better... "To listen is to love."

6. Treasure Hunt

Life is a treasure hunt with diamonds and emeralds strewn along the path, with gold nuggets in the darkest corners, and with brilliant crystals too bright to look at in some places. Most of all are the little pearls in moments of days. The glistening of them as we listen with our hearts open to those who are most difficult for us, the sick, the crippled, the handicapped, the homeless, the abusers, all those the world rejects in its pride. If you are willing to walk along with these, listening, letting others see you as you walk along, not being conscious of their eyes on you, but only listening fully, then you love. As we walk along through life the opportunity is always there to collect these treasures by giving, sharing, encouraging, and accepting others. The biggest and best treasures are found in our acceptance of others.

7. Value Is in the Opposite

All that is seen is not. All that is unseen is. The eye cannot see, nor the ear, hear, love!! I used to think it was a paradox; now I know it's a parallel. Only God is in the opposite and His reflection is in the side where we are. Where we are is not real. We have the power to step across the space, across the interface to the real world.

Driving on the center line will not work; it is the quickest way to death. To turn around you must cross over the line, and to stay you must drive on the road up. U-turns and U-turns and U-turns are going in circles and the cliffs nearby invite disaster as the dizziness comes on. We need to know it is right and good. For many times the fog, snow, cold, heat, and haze keep us from seeing clearly.

8. Conversion

A per/son—part of/the son. All words are plays, pictures, visions of what man sees, wants, dreams, and hopes. They can be twisted, ruined; they can be like a river of love. For some, the words of Jesus are ignored. They harden their hearts. They do not hear. They do not see. To others, his parables are para-blessings. Where do all the words flow from? Through me to you. the source is always the same—God. He takes our mistakes, all mistakes, and in time He makes fertilizer whether we like it or not. Flowers grow out of rocks. The seeds of trees find soil there. The rocks crack and crumble in time as the trees grow, drawing living water from the very rocks. God is good!

9. Home

Where your heart...
Where your treasure lies.

10. Some Words

Written words a prayer do make. From the heart the river flows down the way and through the pen and into the minds and onto hearts. Hearts are the parchment where the words are held and they live and beat and complete the message sending it forth to other hearts.

L	U	C	K		H	O	P	E
i	n	h	i		a	n	o	x
v	d	r	n		v	l	s	p
i	e	i	d		i	y	i	e
n	r	s	n		n		t	c
g		t	e		g		i	t
		's	s				v	a
			s				e	t
								i
								o
								n
								s

11. Inside

Inside the heart is the realm of the kingdom of God, the kingdom inside. To enter this kingdom, there must be love of all creation – myself, others and my enemies. If you have this love, you have everything. The world can no longer hold you. You are alive to the extent you love, to the extent you love yourself because of God's love for you. In acknowledging this love, you allow love to flow in, through, and out to others. Holy means getting it all together so that you are wholly there.

See me in the very air you breathe.
See me in each ray of light.

See me in each fleck of dust.
See me in the pain and smiles.
See me in the clouds above.
See me, for I always see you, and I love you.

12. Morning Thoughts

It's been known a long time that the hours before midnight are the best for sleeping. It has also been known that the time to get up is when you wake in the early morning. Going back to sleep blurs the senses. So, get up when you wake up and pray and work and be alive, even though it may be 4 a.m. The most important work is creativity. It is closer to prayer than some other works if the things created honor God. The next important work is clean up. Clean up is essential. Without it the mind gets cluttered with thoughts of the mess and creativity cannot be renewed as it should.

Chapter V—Life

1. Yours

I was yours to be a friend to or use and discard. What you cannot see is my undiscard-ableness. At first I could not see it either; but then, someone somewhere showed me a mirror inside of them that gave me a better view of me. Someone else's mirror showed me another view and I realized more of me. Now I cannot let you use me, because I am only yours to be a friend to, not ever to use and discard.

2. He Walks Along

He walks along and the trail of his footsteps leaves a path for those who follow along the way.

And as he walks he thinks of his mom how brave she was to allow him to be.

He walks along and the trail of his footsteps leaves a path for those who follow along the way.

3. Trees

Trees trees – they breathe out oxygen. They give us life. They shade and protect us.

Trees trees – they stand so tall. They give us hope. They weather any storms and seasons.

Trees trees – They burn so bright. They give us warmth. They become the logs and kindling of our winters.

Trees trees – They remind us. They are symbols of love. They become for us a source of courage.

Thank God for trees.

4. The Rose
The rose unfolds.
Oh the rose unfolds.
Oh the rose unfolds and the thorns protect it as it grows.
Oh the rose unfolds.
Oh the rose unfolds and it draws from the soil as it goes.
Oh the rose unfolds.
Oh the rose unfolds and the river gives it water as it flows.
Oh the rose unfolds.
Oh the rose unfolds and a fragrance and a beauty it bestows.
Oh the rose unfolds.
Oh the rose unfolds and a story of love is foretold.
Oh the rose unfolds.
Oh the rose unfolds.
Oh the rose unfolds.

5. Luck
Good luck – good <u>l</u>iving <u>u</u>nder <u>C</u>hrist's <u>k</u>indness. Yes, it is good living under Christ's kindness. Let words used every day remind you of <u>The Word</u>.

6. Fear
FEAR – f-false e-energy a-arresting r-reality.

7. Flowers
   Fortunately we are not responsible for unfolding flowers. It's the same for finding spouses. LET GO, LET GOD.

8. Masses
How quickly it passes,
As fast as the grasses.
They used to be masses
and now turned to gasses.

How easy to jest,
Along with the rest.
The ones who are messed
Often become best.

   If I sit and try to write it's no good. The time to write has its place.
   There's a right time for everything...a time to be born, a time to die, a time to plant, a time to harvest,...
   [Ecclesiastes 3.1-8]

9. Fall
   The leaves fall down like rain in the breeze. The feeling of time passing is overwhelming. The feelings of sadness are there too, the mysterious messages of love. He is so present in His creation. He is so very deep in His thoughts. His simplicity is magnificent. His love is

unlimited. He is the same in all of His seasons. Thank you, God, for loving us.

10. Living

We have to learn certain things as we live. They have to do with practical survival in our world. They relate to physical things like eating and sleeping, what and where. We are familiar with most of them. The others we learn as we live along. They are all temporary things that can lead to nowhere. If you put yourself into them it's a waste. In order to really be alive you must learn:
1. You are special; 2. You are the controller of you; 3.Your habits are dangerous; they can mar the adventure. 4. In giving up things is tremendous growth. 5. To lift up others is a source of inner beauty.
Patterns and habits break or not. Growth is a stretching, breaking experience. I am the only me that is. There is no other. I am separate, yet deep inside of me is a knowing. It says these people all around are needing to know me, needing my unique beauty. Each person I meet is changed because they have seen me. Each person I meet either becomes more or less because of me. I hold the power to increase love in the world. By love I mean kindness, happiness, friendship, trust, joy. Or, I can cause, by the power in me, division, disaster, pain, hurt, turmoil, and a foulness of speech that can make others feel worthless. I am responsible for the putting down or the lifting up of the others in each moment of my life. I can change. I can

become new. Each breath I breathe gives me another chance, makes me new, and gives me a new start.

It's a beautiful new day. Here we all are new, free, and alive. No matter what went on yesterday, today is new, a day to be all that I can be. Moments are adventures.

11. Moments

The sands of time...so many little rocks...a rock at a time...A MOMENT AT A TIME...in silence, the truth lights the room. Each moment is a gentle lifting and storing for we must one day see that light comes from the moments. It's not sand we are dealing with. Those are not just rocks, but diamonds and rubies and emeralds, precious moments of kindness and truth. This is the source of light, the burning love that shines from within these so-called sands of time. So right now is the time to get together, to acknowledge the power of the friendship we have need and hope for, to acknowledge the power of love that brings us flowers out of manure and who makes a wonder of a night sky and the oceans and the trees. We need to stop and look and really see. Thank you GOD! Thank you Lord Jesus! Thank you for your love and mercy. IT'S NOT HOW YOU FEEL. It's what you do. Doing takes deciding, thinking, and then acting. If you choose sad you will think and do sad. Reactions are in need of thought. Because to be really human, really aware, we must take the moments seriously. They affect each and every person in our lives, especially us. Moments, sands of time, grains of wheat, seeds of thought...seeds, stars, sand grains, wheat grains, MOMENTS! In each moment of our lives, the people and the things, all of them, little and big, are important.

We need to slow down in a natural way and get to a quiet place away from people and things. We need to get clarity inside of us. Like clearing the screen on a computer. Each day we need this quiet clear time. The most beautiful living takes place in these times of clear consciousness, in acknowledging our love of all and letting go of hate and anger. No other living person can give you love. You have to discover it inside your own heart. Until you find love in your heart you cannot accept it from others. Love is a flowing, a going on forever and forever. YOU MUST LOOK INSIDE.

12. Trip

When you take a bus do you have concern for the bus after the trip is completed? When you take a taxi in the city do you care where it goes after it lets you off? Why then do you worry about what you wear or what special things you eat? As long as it works well and is clean you could care less about the taxi or bus. We are travelers to the real, through the unreal. We carry the real deep inside. It is an inside trip we are on.

14. The Choice

In the calm still of early morning, before the sunrise, when the stillness of anticipation was on the land, a voice broke the light. Man became aware of the existence of good and evil, and because of words man became blinded to his unique beauty and his unique gifts. Man then decided not to love. He made a mistake and lost sight of his lovableness. He lost sight of the tremendous love of God for him. The creator let him be and continues to this day to pour on him unlimited beauty, unlimited power, unlimited love, hoping that he will close the doors to blackness and open wide the doors to light so that he can clearly see in his heart.

15. The Castle

In the castle where he lives, man has a treasure room and a dungeon. As he lives he chooses the doors he wishes to keep open. He shares from the rooms within himself. So open your treasure room and share the reality of you. Long, long ago, when all was brand new and absolutely pure, man became aware of the existence of good and evil, and because of words, he became blinded to the unique beauty of each gift and he chose to destroy rather than to love. Fear needs words; words are the fuel of fear. Fear is imprisoned without words. Love can stand alone without sound. Fear needs sound to survive. Fear is a physical thing. Fear is a mental thing. Love is of the heart. Fear is shallow. Love is deep.

16. Face to Face

If a man makes a million dollars and gives it to his son, he ruins his own son. If a father loves his son it is real! It is all they have to give each other. It is enough, like a vessel full to the brim. Space is the interface place. There is no other place. There is only the interface: God and man face to face, in love for eternity with unlimited eternal love, one to one, all one to all, all all to all. Love is not separate, it is one. It is like the water smooth and level open to all. Only the damned hold back the waters of love. The mind will do whatever the self commands. The mind is the servant of self. The mind will work in all possible ways to support whatever the self thinks it is. Rethink! Rethink!

17. Gifts

These treasures are all we really have to give each other. These are all that is. People are! Love is! All things serve. Without people and without love, the world has no meaning at all. God's creation is to show in unlimited ways His eternal and unlimited love for each of us. None of this is yours alone or mine alone. Generations come and go and this treasure goes on, uncollectable, uncontrollable, except for a short time. And yet we say this is ours and that is mine.

18. Seamless

"Put aside the things of the world and come follow me…" "Be faithful to me in little things and I will give you bigger things to be faithful in." Paraphrased—"Give up little things for me and I will give you bigger things to give up." A man without habits can be free to really be in the moments of his life. A person must cut out habits for they are not of love and therefore dead. A man without habits is free to follow his own inner lights and choose the routines of his daily living unobstructed by things. Routines and patterns we all have and some are necessary to fulfill the work set before us. Habits are thing-based. We allow them to take control of our lives. They can grow and increase and take over all the living moments we have. Habits imprison the spirit of goodness in a person and cause that person to not really be. Many people are so caught up in their habits that for all intents and purposed they are dead. They cast lots for a seamless robe, the robe of a man without habits.

19. On Growing

Eight years and eight years and eight years makes a man. Who in late years will be...It takes eight years and eight years and eight years plus late years to learn the meaning that fills the heart of a man. In the land of the heart there is no limit to growth.

Chapter VI—Seeds

1. Man Is Responsible

     Dignity...The dignity of man is tied to his seeds, the most valuable gift man has received. Oh man how simple it is. What farmer would plant his seeds on another farmer's land? What farmer would plant his seeds in poisoned land? What farmer would throw his seeds down the toilet? What farmer would kill each little plant as it begins to grow? The seeds of man are each unique and eternal. Only God's forgiveness can save man from his failures regarding seeds. Each child will be born. The prayer says, "Thy will be done." Tell me is there a farmer that does not desire the fertility of each and every seed? God is the farmer, the great farmer who can and will make each seed fertile.

2. The Farmer

     A farmer, a man – the garden, the earth – the fruit, man's child. God calls to you, oh man! His call is simple and pure and good...Oh man, not in the soft petals of the flower, not in the handle of the plow, not in the bowels of the earth, or in the beast that plows as helper, but simply and most beautifully in the full rich soil where they belong. The seeds in the sack will never be lost. God knows their true value like oil. They must be kept ready in the lamps.

3. Seeds

     We ordered seeds today, vegetables, trees, and flowers. In the spring we will plant many things. With God there is no season. The seeds most important are seeds of the heart, seeds of patience, kindness, peace, and love. Another thing about His seeds is they go on forever. They never die. They grow and grow and grow. The only reason the plants of God's seeds have not taken over the world is fear. Fear is like a weed that chokes not only little plants but even full grown plants.

4. Flowers

When we look at a flower what do we see? The color, shape, size, length of stem, the green of the leaves, the leaves closeness to the bloom or the thorns and spikes on the stem. We look first to see the beauty of the bloom and rightly so. If we had looked before we would have seen the closed bud or, before that, the little pregnant nodule on the stem. Or back, way back, we would have seen the struggling through the dirt and rocks, the fertilizer, the bugs that infested the scene, the winds and rain, the coldness of winter and the heat of the sun, the days and days of waiting, the closeness of the hoe and the plow, the feet that walked heavily along the rows, the prison-like rows, setting row after row, the hopelessness, and the pain of growing. And, back to the seed being buried down down, shoved into the dirt with no hope from outside. The waiting in darkness.

5. Harvest

A farmer plants and hopes for rain and cares for the plants and waits for the harvest. It's that simple even more. A farmer plants on his own land so he knows the harvest is his. He has a written deed. It's that simple. Children are the greatest harvest for man. Marriage is a written deed. A real man cares for his woman like a farmer cares for his land. He marries her.

6. He Grows

He was a wind, when first he gusted, carrying a little sack out across the plain. He was full of life, fun and games, eager to learn from each one he met. When he became twelve, he first noticed the slant of the ground. It was an incline. Time passed and it became clearer. When he first noticed the hills he was fourteen and soon the force winds began. With his little sack he moved into a different world. He began to realize what the seeds in the sack were for; the quest had begun. At eighteen he knew that it was from among the hills he was to choose a place to plant. But beyond the hills he could see the mountains as the sun shone on their flat rock surfaces and their snow caps. He was drawn toward the mountains and drawn toward the hills. The decision faced him. He decided.

7. She Grows

She was a hill and throughout the ages she was formed and clothed with flowers and green of all different shades for all the seasons. She lay there in all her splendor of wild flowers and leaves of green. She held herself strong against the wending winds who attempted to buffet her. They made but little ripples in the flower petals.

8. Marriage

Then he came, the waiting time was over, and the seeds went into her soil. Life and love met and became one forever looking always together toward the mountains from where the living water flows. Oh man it is that simple. The seasons pass and renew and renew and renew. Life and love are one forever.

Chapter VII—Stories

1. Tables

They sat there across the room, three people . . . the tables square, the chairs of wood with rounded backs . . . separate tables, alone, looking out of windows at the world of cars, building, and people.

I have watched them and I have wanted them to know each other. One woman, two men, and then a friend came in and sat across from one guy. The woman received her meal. Lunchtime started. Others came and it was past. The moment lost in the maze of moments but not for me. I have it stored away in my mind. To be alone, it is a good file, a necessary file of creation, dreams, hopes and interlaced with LOVE.

2. The City

The city was magnificent . . . the buildings shining against the night sky . . . the freeway sparkling as it curved above and turned along the coast. From above, way up on the hills, where you could see clearly the bridges and buildings, it was a beautiful sight, like a woman all decked out in diamonds. In reality, it was like a prostitute whose bathing beauty is covered by jewels, while hidden beneath are the diseases of wanton sicknesses and perversion. Oh! San Francisco for the sake of your name's sake, clean up or disappear under the waves. Waves of rotten disease.

3. High School

A lifetime in four years. What is it meant to be? What is it really in our society? This difference is the cause of our troubles with schools. We are like clay, when young and youthful we are moldable, movable, almost meltable.

As we run into the hard realities of life and suffer the disillusionment, the hard knives, and the preheat of other people's hells. We get hardened. The vast majority of almost all high school students in the ninth, tenth, and eleventh grades are not so hard that melting might still be possible. Some are hard even down into the sixth, seventh, and eighth grades. Yes, some are crystallized very young. This hardness is of the heart and all of our troubles as individuals and nations comes from this hardening of hearts. Very young people have soft hearts, almost liquid. The tears and the laughter flow easily. The sharings are true and real. As we grow we run into hardeners, melters, and crackers. Love is like the tears of living water. Did you know that the purest water, in you, is tears?

High school starts as a very scary situation for most ninth graders. For some, embarrassment is the fear that dominates them. Others are too young to realize embarrassment. Few have grown past it, very few. So the ninth grader comes into a scene that is full of seemingly adult people. The ninth grader assumes that these people know all about life. Know all about life means they know all about sex. The seniors look like they know all about everything and they at eighteen act like they do. This complicates the problem further. The teachers know all this and they assume the ninth grader does too. So because of these assumptions, at least a year or two of valuable thinking is lost. Valuable thinking is the thinking about self. Yes, high school has only two lessons: first, to know and to love yourself, and second, to wait and learn as much as possible so that you can be the best you possibly can for others. Nothing comes from any high school lessons unless it pertains to the heart.

The science classes, the math classes, the English classes, the teams, the band, and the games, all have meaning only if the student eventually applies them to learning about and giving to others himself. We are like rivers, we people. We flow out in giving or we get dammed up and turn into stale ebb tides filled with our scum-like collections. To kill the morbid parts of our situations we try pouring poisons on. Only in flowing out can we get to the valley and become the lake together. The world goes on using and abusing our talents, drying up our tears, covering over and sealing off our realities.

We who enter high school are searching for knowledge of love. We are striving to be better lovers in the world. We are blind. We are small. We need a hand. We need to be lifted up and accepted and nourished like a flower.

Teachers are the keys. Teachers who accept and understand and love are bringing about the softening, the melting, and the cracking of hearts. Love is the ultimate lesson. Love cannot flow from hard hearts. In high school we may or may not learn one of the greatest lessons to learn: "Wait and know that love is not a physical thing."

Love goes beyond physical. Its boundaries have no limit. We can only vaguely see it. Yet it stands boldly in front of us every day and night. If we saw it once nothing could ever compare. It would be our constant obsession. It calls us saying, "I am the unacceptable one, see me, reach out to me. I need your love more than all the rest."

4. Broken Hearts

Inside of you and me it's good. The coatings are flaky, crusty, and hard. The cracking of the shell is like the breaking of a heart. Love cannot get out of a hard heart. Only broken hearts know what love is. Only tears can melt away the fibers that keep us locked away in fear. To be free, okay, alive, we must be standing in the middle of the stream like a rock, for the sake of others who need us to be there. A strong person is one who can step away forever from addictions of all kinds, and look at the world as a free person unchained to things.

5. Convert

He was about fourteen when he thought of it. Why he did is a mystery, but he did. I guess it was just after he saw the puppies get born. After that he changed, an amazing change. Even though she was flat out drunk he would smile at her with kindness mixed with lots of pity. He cleaned up the place, the inside first then the yard. With money he got from small jobs he bought paint and a brush. He painted the old rented house where they lived. The other kids laughed at him at first but when he said nothing they were quiet. No telling what they thought.

His whole life changed after that. He went to school and studied. He even did all the homework. When he graduated from high school he got a government grant and went to the junior college. His mom never changed; she still had her bottles and her bums. He never complained. He kept the place clean for her, he cooked for her. He worked hard and studied. He had no time for his so-called friends. They didn't change much. He received orientation papers from several universities. One day he moved away in a rented truck; where he went nobody knew.

6. The Search

When I was very young my mom was the most important person to me. About the age of four I became conscious of my dad. What dad said got done. So I thought dad was perfect. He could do no wrong. If he hit me I was bad, never him. I made him my God. When I got older I became conscious of Dad's faults but I held on to the hope that he was perfect. He just was not.

Through fourteen, fifteen, sixteen, seventeen, and eighteen, I grew. I started to search for the perfect one. I looked for a perfect friend. Now I know I was really searching for someone inside of me. I was searching for God, the good that is in me, the love that is me, and not me but something more.

The search continues. To believe is not enough. We want to KNOW!!

7. Inside Outside

The trip inside is never cold and never too hot. It has no high mountains and it has no fertile valleys. It is mostly barren and plain and sometimes seems dull and boring. The fuel for this trip comes from deep inside much like the fuel of the world. However this fuel is uncontainable and invisible. It is similar to electricity, magnetism, or gravity. It gently pushes and pushes. The less we hold back the faster and farther it will take us.

8. You

Hey! There is no other you!!! Are the windows open? Are the paths smooth? Do you know the key that opens the door to your heart? Each breath is a new life, a new start. Don't look back, the payments due will come up to you as you live. Look NOW!!! BE in each moment, all that you can be. See clearly the good and all its flavor, style, and color.

9. Choose

Dear people, please listen. You need to know how wonderful you are, each of you right now. You have the power to clean up, straighten out and BE. To live is a decision. So decide to love yourself enough to let go of, to get free of whatever keeps you from being YOU. Choose life. Choose marriage. Choose children. Let fear be damned.

10. Wasted

Yes, wasted all the years of my high school, because being in fear I was not present to the others who surrounded me each day. Wasted were many opportunities to be a friend to those who most needed me. AND WHERE WAS I? Lost in a maze of who am I? Why was I born? Why do I have to look the way I do? Why is the family the way it is? Poor me!!! Poor poor poor meeeeeee!!! Why can't I have a dad like Jimmy? Why is my mom so messed up? Why didn't I come from a really neat family? Why does everyone think my family is so great? Can't they see the rules make it impossible for me to really be . . .? Why doesn't everyone smoke like me? Why can't I dump this junk I am using? Where am I going with my life? Where, Why, Who, What, When, Which, How??? And would you believe that. "How?" is the beginning of all the answers. The Indians looked deep into the eyes of the white man and said HOW!

11. Waste

A man makes something with his hands and part of his life goes into the making. If a man's life is valuable then the things he makes have part of that same value. When we destroy we better be sure that the things we destroy do not waste the lifetime of our father and mother and all the other creators of the things and ideas that we use and need every day.

12. Dump

To the dump, to the dump, to the dump, dump, dump . . .
To collect stuff . . . JOY IS IN THE OPPOSITE . . .
Fertilizer is necessary, without it the tree itself cannot grow and bear fruit.

13. Captain

He was the captain of his ship and he wrote in her log. He wrote also more each day in another book. In his writings he told of life, of his hopes and dreams and even more. He told of the way he saw the world and he told of his love for life. He told of these in a unique and wonderful way. Yes, in such a way that has never been told before and will never be told again.

It was a terrible storm that night; way out to sea they were. All was lost from sight, never to be seen again. Those words he wrote since they were written down—are they safe and sound?

14. Toy

All he ever had was a few rags. The only food he had ever eaten was scraps from the trash. One day an old man gave him a small toy which he carried with him everywhere. He heard but did not understand the words.

Suffer the little children to come unto me. Without hesitation he gave his toy to Jesus.

15. Danger
The danger
Yes, there is a danger.
The danger, the danger
To never confront evil in any shape or form
Yes, to never confront evil in any shape or form

The danger
Yes, there is a danger.
The danger, the danger
To think you are any better in any shape or form

The danger
Yes, there is a danger.
The danger, the danger
To never confront evil in any shape or form.

16. Dream
Hey dream, hey dream, hey dream because in your dreaming you show faith.
Hey dream, hey dream, hey dream because in your dreaming you show hope.
Hey dream, hey dream, hey dream because in your dreaming you show love.
Hey dream, because in your dreaming you show faith, hope, and love.

17. Playmate

Why don't you come out and play? I see your face in the window.

Oh why don't you come out and play? Your face was smiling today.

I am here in the lot across the street. Me and my imaginary friends. I asked your mom if you could play. She told me your name. I saw you again today in the window.

Hey Jody! Why don't you come out and play? I am lonely.

Today I came and you were not there. Oh Jody! Your mother told me you died. WHY?

18. Little Kids

Little kids are the neatest people around. They forgive and forget. They share and receive. They are open and vulnerable. They allow their enthusiasm to show and that's rare indeed. Be a little kid today in your heart.

19. Off to Work
Off to work
Sure can't shirk
Get on shoes
And pants and shirt

Put on coat
Go outside
Start that truck

Battery's dead

Push it down
The muddy road
Yell for help
And let out the clutch
Nothing

Kids come runnin'
Mama too
Everybody push
And watch the puddles
Catch your breath
Or you'll turn blue

On down the road
Into the chuck holes
Bump bump bump
There goes the tire
No school
No work

Chapter VIII—Teacher

1. Teacher

As a teacher, I reflect in a moment some words for each and every person in all the classes I have ever taught.

What an honor and a joy to have you in my class to be able to associate with the beauty and the intelligence that is you! What an honor and a joy to have you in my class to be able to share with you in the moments, the inspirations that flow from my heart. What an honor and a joy to have you in my class to be able to just be in your presence amid the noise and confusion of life!

2. Teach

You who teach have a special privilege. Before you is the most beautiful scene.
"To listen is to love" and those before you are a room full of lovers awaiting your every word. Be aware of each and every one of them. Learn quickly each one's name and look into their eyes. Give to each your acceptance. Allow each to be as he or she is. Let the light of your acceptance and love be the example. Love them back. Listen to them.

3. The World

The world of mankind denies its true father and puts distractions in the way of truth. Many young people look for a father in each other or in a singer or an older man or woman or in their own father. They look for direction needed for the second lifetime, emotional direction. Unless they find God, the real Father of mankind, they float along at seventeen, eighteen, nineteen, twenty, and twenty-one, and on because they are not born again out of the first lifetime and in many ways they are living dead. They devise a meaning for life that leaves out God and true love.

4. Lifetimes

How many ways can we say the truth? In all generations, in every culture it has been spoken. It is buried within us. We reflect the truth like a mirror and like a mirror we have another side that is covered over, buried.

Everything in our lives has value. The most valuable things are buried in dirt...gold and diamonds, pain and past evil, anguish, hurt, and rejection. All of these can be more valuable than the good things that happen to us. It's like we have two times of life learning: The first is learning and growing physically. The second is learning to grow emotionally and spiritually, to forgive and give, to accept and to love. We each have growing to do in each lifetime. We are all growing physically, emotionally, and spiritually. We are learning, always learning.

5. Love and Growing

Love is Learning of Values Eternal. WE GROW FROM 0 TO 11, AND FROM 12 TO 20, AND FROM 20 ON. When we were young we looked to our mother and then our father. As time passed we grew to realize that we too would have to leave.

Having a good family is ideal. It is true and perfect and ideal, but many of us did not come from families that were ideal. Many of us came from untrue places and unreal parents who put us away in orphanages, never wanting to see us again. Actually never wanted us to be born and rejected us in the womb. So our birth to ten was filled with drunkenness, divorce, horrors, pains, and fears. Some of us who came from fairly good families quickly rejected all the values we learned and sought to find other ways.

6. Stop Now, Step Back

Stop Now, step back, get alone, decide to change, and look inside...important? STUDIES...preparation for success...hard work to become a professional, to set the correct image, to be known as or for or just known....This drive, this striving, uses up the energy of living and time passes. In the time that passes people also pass and become forgotten or driven from mind because the work is all-encompassing. The driving toward the goal becomes the obsession. The life energy is consumed in the striving and love is lost in the complex maze of timing and doing. Reality is obscured and the idol, whatever it may be, becomes the god. The God of love is lost to things, and it is forgotten that "the exalted shall be humbled and the humble exalted." A poor man in love is a king of all he surveys.

7. Today

In a garden of roses surrounded by fields of flowers, the people's faces are the blooms. Some are perfect. Some are drooping. Some are clinging to places where little soil and sparse water can be found. Some have been trampled in the dark of night. Some are in neat orderly flower boxes. Some have been contaminated by smoke and chemicals. All need loving care and acceptance. All need fresh water. All need kind words and soft music. Many need to be lifted up and transplanted by the wind to fertile soil near the bank of a stream. All need love; the love that is friendship clean and pure. Sometimes I think people could change by deciding, and I know it's true. But it takes such tremendous energy and power to do this. To overcome the soil, the plant needs to do this too. Otherwise the plant can't grow.

The soil is sometimes full of chemicals and nicotine and caffeine and all sorts of other weeds and leaves, with its nature, its dust, the slugs, pincher bugs, lizards, snakes, and all sorts of bugs that live there. The plant must lift itself above the soil and reach out toward the sun. People are so much like plants they get bogged down stuck in places, crawled on, bitten, covered with dirt and slime. To grow they must lift themselves up toward the son. Only you can lift yourself up. It's the power within that can help you to change. Nothing from outside is lasting. No chemicals, no touch, can bring you happiness that lasts.

Look inside, it's the heart part. The heart part is true. True friends will lead you to truth. True friends bring true gifts like flowers. Never will a true friend bring you to chemicals or drugs. True friends lift you up. Never would a true friend bring you down, down to the dirt and the manure and the biting bugs in the sickness and slime.

Remember what flowers do to manure. They change it to fertilizer. It's not easy to change. It takes tremendous energy and power. But you have it, all the power you need.

8. Age

Age is not. The container is like the package, the wrapping, and the box. It falls away and what's really important is what's inside. The self lives on. It is the real you, the heart of you.

We play good tapes and bad tapes; our computer can be lied to; it can have a program that gets altered. Programming is putting in the truth in youth, putting in the true facts about life, and putting in love and acceptance. The computer accepts everything, lies or truth. It is open to all input. So, if the self thinks that it is an addict and presses the buttons to back up its addictions or desires, the computer will immediately bring forth pictures, tapes, and printouts to back these things. If the self receives messages that it is no good, something special happens; red lights flash an error. For the heart of the self is good.

9. Peace

Stand up for peace. Fight for it, but not as the world fights. With words yes, with spoken and written and taped words, calmly, stand up for peace without a club in your hand. If they kill you or club you down, keep standing as long as you can. Drag yourself up. Stand up for peace or peace will be lost in the arsenals and prisons and graves of this world. If we do not stand up for peace we are already dead.

10. Patient

To be patient sometimes it is necessary to concentrate yourself into another place.

Shutting out the incoming words; pains, rains, stains, and drains, and concentrate on God, Fixing His positive world of loving hearts into everything. Allowing no wound or touch or feeling to penetrate.

Placing a look of peace on your face.

And, sitting oblivious to one and all,

Yet, looking open and in a listening stance.

While really only listening to an inner voice of angels and flowing streams of love.

11. Waiting

It is a time of waiting. The minutes seem in need of filling, yet they are full for me. It is a time of patience. The minutes are difficult and trying, yet they are good for me. It is a time of growing. The minutes are threaded with some pain, yet they are bringing to me love. It is a time to be loving. The minutes are full of chances for acceptance by me. It is a time of really learning. The minutes are lessons in the art of loving, yet they are difficult for me. It is good to be quiet unless what you are going to say wipes out fear or lifts up your listener. It is best to listen and hope, because love is in the listening, like the leaves and the streams.

12. Unreal

The living dead create a false world and continue it and grow in it. It is a world where money or things become the father, the idol, and this is a world as we see it today. It is fabricated and unreal. The money, the cars, the houses, the factories, all of it, is unreal; but it's so tremendous a distraction that when it teaches all it knows, people follow. Physical is where the world is. It is back in the first lifetime, but now these are grown men and women, and they are playing nasty, playing with their toys and games. Lost is the curiosity of the growing child. Curiosity and enthusiasm have been replaced by lust and greed. Last year our world spent 90 million dollars on eye makeup alone and when you get into playing soldier it's sad and sick and such a waste of love.

13. Hey

You, each of you, is neat and nice and fine. Imagine us on an adventure. Who among us would provide food and who would be the ones who carried the packs? Who would plan the paths and who would be there to take away the fear of going on and who would remove the rocks and trees out of our way and who would sew together the skins of fur to keep us warm and who would go out in front way ahead to scout the way and who would protect us at the sides and who would be the last in the line to protect from attack and to urge the stragglers on? These are the jobs you will have to do to be alive. All others head to nowhere, to a seat in front of a box with a can of beer in hand, to a lonely room where habits crowd in and destroy.

The adventure continues. The going on, the real living, leaves no room for fear and death. The real living calls to us, and asks us to put aside pleasures, to put aside comfort to put aside things and to go out into the world of adventure; helping, curing, protecting, and lifting up. We want to be those who really live, not those who die in their habits, lonely because they were afraid and lonely because they continued to allow themselves to be carried away in the pleasures that end empty like smoke or vomit.

To really be alive we must get beyond ourselves. We must acknowledge our goodness and our deep love for others, then deny pleasure and look to others' needs, helping them get past the whining and self-pity, the poor me. We must be standing strong. We must walk away from some situations and stand alone if necessary. We must look inside to the source of our power. Look inside and follow our heart instead of our mind and body.

14. Some Facts of Life

"To be or not to be"...real. Whatever you give away you get to keep. If you give away kindness you get to keep kindness. So give away kindness, smiles, peace, reality, and joy. But if you lock in kindness, out of fear, and you hold back trust, out of mistrust, and you do not smile because it's not macho and you keep away from peace because you feel hate inside and you are not real because reality is too vulnerable, too scary, and you do not let joy out because only kids, very little kids, do that, then you can never have kindness, smiles, peace, reality, or joy. Because "WHAT YOU GIVE AWAY YOU GET TO KEEP." Love is calling you to be real, true and good. You cannot do bad unless first you rationalize it into good. You know how it is, you need to blame someone else.

    I love you. My loving you does not mean I am going to support you; it means that I have hope for you, hope that sees you standing strong for yourself. When you see a male deer standing on a hill near the edge of the forest, quiet, alert, and strong, he is like a symbol of manhood. When you see a man standing holding a small child in his arms, he is a symbol of strength and power. A priest holding the chalice up in the consecration of the mass is also a symbol of strength and power. We are born to be kind, to be thoughtful, to be good and positive and, yes, strong. Kindness, truth, realness, these are life giving things.

    Reality is alive. Everything in the world has lines in it. Flowing lines. Rocks, leaves, water in a pond, the ocean, the clouds, stars, and faces of people, all have lines of flowing. As you live along you get lines etched into your face. If you practice kindness the lines become soft and kind and the smile is like a gift full of trust. If you practice selfishness the lines become hard and sharp and the smile is a sneer full of mistrust.

15. Two Choices Only

Man has really only two choices; all other paths lead to nothingness, emptiness, and prisons. Man's two choices are: The first choice is to remain celibate, single, placing all hope in God, then, go out into the world, doing good to all, being strong for the weak and being able to create beauty, dreams, and hope for others, and to console and explain and revive the true spirit of love in their hearts. The second choice is to wait upon God, who will send a spouse, and to live with that spouse in purity and fruitfulness with complete trust in God the Father's love. This truth cannot be denied. It is certain because we have it carved into our hearts. If we as children learn to be untrue, when we see the truth we will know it like a light in the darkness. It is carved into us. Flow on, oh nature, flow on!

16. Reality

Gravestone…"died at 30 buried at 60"…to be or not to be is the question. Further…deeper…you are alive to the extent you live in the hearts of others. And you give life to the extent you can actually become a person who is a friend to everyone he meets. Caring is a matter of life and death, caring with each breath, caring with each word, and caring in each moment.

Notice yourself. Become aware of the goodness that is you. You are in-between. You are in a time of waiting. Many more waiting times are before you. We are like plants, CRAZY, but yes we are like plants—fertile soil, rocks, fertilizer. The ideas you think and dream will never be thought of or dreamed of again by anyone in all of time. You are unique, beautiful. Do you want to be big, bigger, stronger than it's even possible?

God is in the opposite. The world sees the reflection—His trees, His lakes, His oceans, but God is in the opposite – love is in the opposite. Love is a dirty diaper at 3 a.m. The lover is the changer. Love is a sink crammed with dirty, sticky dishes. The lover is there washing away without being asked. Cinderella was a lover…. What you give away you get to keep. If you give away love you get to keep love….

Love is doing the task set before you, the math, the English, the social studies, the sweeping of floors, the washing of dishes, the laundry. Love is kind even to enemies. Love is never ridiculing even in fun. Love lifts the other person up. Love makes a king of kings out of a man despised by his own people. Love denies itself cigarettes and booze. Love is clean. Love is warm. Love is a friend to the one who is most ridiculed. Love walks together with the lowly. LOVE IS! Thank God!

I love you because you are, not because of any way you look or anything you do. I love you because I look inside of me and find you there, you in your embarrassment and fear, you in your hopes and dreams, you in your individual beauty....

17. Lamp Oil

If the oil in the lamps is the energy of love in hearts, and Jesus is our spouse whom we need to save and preserve our love for, then wasting anything is not good. The love energy is the only important resource we have. Men are the spiritual leaders of family. Family needs the love of its man. A love that is sensitive, aware, and in the moments. If we equate the sperm or seed of man to the oil in the lamps, men and women become clearly responsible for the preservation of the oil.

The world makes women the symbol of love. The oil is burnt in adoration of women and also in unnatural ways...making a god out of the physical and making an offering of energy, energy meant for Christ. The energy of love is needed in the world by people searching for Christ. These people are calling out to us to be conscious, awake, and a light for them. The oil in the lamps keep our light burning in a dark world. The wick in our lamps is Christ himself. He feeds us, we must save our oil, so that when the time is right we will burn brightly in love for those who need us, those lost in the darkness. Celibacy is a call to brightness, a call to be a light brighter for others, a call to love Christ. The wasting and the spilling of the energy that is life's source is a waste of life itself.

No oil in a lamp means no light, a light which the world needs desperately to combat the darkness. A priest is by far an important part of the Kingdom of God. A priest is an emissary of heaven in the world. A priest not only can produce the food necessary, which is the wick of the lamp, he is also a lamp full of oil for those in need of light. We all need light. The light of each other's love. For a man to be called to the priesthood is a call from beyond the world...a call to be...really be! Many are called to be, but few become...become a source of love in the world...a direct source of God's love in the world. The container is weak. The oil is extremely valuable. We are all priests in this way, the way of the oil and the lamp. Only an ordained priest is the source of the food needed (the wick needed) that holds the oil to be fed into the flame from inside the lamp, the flame of love.

18. Modern Man

The body is a container, fantastic, amazing, beautiful in structure, similar yet unique, magnificent! Imagine it as a room. The mind is a machine, fantastic, amazing capacity, similar yet unique, magnificent! Imagine that it is a computer. So, in the room with the computer is YOU. Who, though, is you? Who is me?...Let's say "a SELF." The person in the room with the computer is your self. The self is like a light or a flame. The video screen of the computer is connected to our eyes. Look into the eyes; the eyes have it.

We and we alone can push our own computer buttons. NOW! with your eyes closed, look inside your room and see yourself as a light, a light that can move around and reach out. Make your light as bright as you can. This is you. This is the fire of your love (pure).

It is impossible for anyone to get into your room or to press your buttons...with one exception...God can enter through the door of your room. He stands knocking. He knows all the right buttons which are special for creating the most magnificent you.

19. Today

Each hour, minute, second is once in a lifetime for each of us...ONCE IN A LIFETIME! To live we must consider important all the happenings of the moments. To actually be real we must live life down to each five minutes at a time. We have to shut out anxiety, fear, worry, embarrassment and guilt. We must be in the here and the now to feel the environment and all that's in it. This is not easy. If we do this we find ourselves in a place that is all adventure. The people become clearly defined and some of the quiet people shine like bright lights. Some of the things to do are such a waste of time, but we can handle it because we only have five minutes and five minutes and then five minutes. So we can do the work set there before us carefully and do it the best we can.

In this clarity, we may be tempted to look at what we see and think "how boring"... "This is living? Ugh!" But, when we do this, we are not really into the whole of the five minutes because we miss the fact that the pencil or pen in our hand was made out of love and the clothes we wear were made out of love and the people around us were created out of love. Our task is to accept out of love. The author who is love will see us in our clarity and increase our power to be. The energy that keeps the stars where they are is made out of love. Just five minutes is all we have and the work before us is the work to be done. The direction is all worked out. The people will be there at the right time. The time for each thing will happen. No one can pry open a rose and come to the fullness the rose was meant to have in time.

Chapter IX—Mary

1. Family

Father, mother, sons and daughters—in a family, who is the heir apparent? The #1 son. And, the #1 son is to be an example for all sons and daughters that follow. The children in need go to the mother, who, if necessary, intercedes for them to the father. The kingdom of heaven is a kingdom for the children of God...the family whose father is God. The mother of God is there to intercede for us. Pray to her for help. She is the mother of mercy.

2. Mother

She brings to us her baby, just born, and offers to let us hold him...we the shepherds of the hills, we the travelers from afar, we the prostitutes, the murderers, the diseased, the crippled, the sick, the despondent. She, like Abraham, stepped up to the altar; only this time the sacrifice is completed. She is magnificent in God's eyes, never to be forgotten.

3. Mary

As we read Isaiah, chapter 7, verses 14, 15, and 16, we begin to see clearly the importance of Mary in our Father's plan. She was the first teacher of the boy Jesus. She was chosen before all others to be the mother of God. The world rejected her; she was an unwed mother **(pregnant woman, actually)** in the days when this meant being stoned to death. Joseph would have failed to stand by her if an angel had not set him straight. She stood there to the very end. She came first with him and always will. If you do not believe this, it is sad. It is written of her that she crushed the head of the snake. The devil cannot stand in the light of Mary's love. She is, and always will be, the mother of God.

It's so easy for the people of today to ignore the place of the mother of God. We have to think of our own mothers to appreciate the love that Jesus has for his mom. Those who ignore her, ignore Him.

4. Hope

The hope for our children...the idea that dollars will help them when inside we know, yes know, that the path of dollars is an illusion and that reality is knowing our value is based on love...our ability to love in all situations...in poverty and in sorrow of the people we love dying and in pain, our own pain and each other's pain...knowing that the moments count, the moments which can become buried in thoughts of land and adventure...while we get so unconscious of the little lovers who come near us searching for someone to say, "You're OK," "You are fantastic."

5. Habits

"Be faithful to me in little things and I will give you bigger things." Can you change? Habits are tapes. Addictions are printouts with video displays and voice capability. Can we change?... Yes, we tape over. We reprogram. We plug the holes up and run it back through on record—play. We make a new sound and a new picture for the screen. Throughout history, we have examples of lives on tape and on screen and in print. The same things have happened to others before. Some died. Some decided to tape over, to start over, to erase the tapes and use the space again for better living. Our computer has plenty of space but little time. So, we cannot wait to do this taping. The self goes on striving to be all that it believes itself to be. It cannot die. It beams on like a beacon light. It can be covered over though, lost in stacks of useless tapes. There is a gravestone that says, "DIED AT 30, BURIED AT 60," buried in old tapes or new tapes that repeat and repeat and repeat. Some people today die at fourteen or fifteen. They cover over, with guilt tapes and fear tapes or anger tapes, the very flame of their real self.

6. Tapes

We have tapes on preferences, tapes on actions of necessity, tapes on daily living tasks, reaction tapes, rejection tapes, happy tapes, sad tapes, response tapes, "how to" tapes, that include all the abstract things as well as concrete things. We have tapes on every conceivable circumstance that we have experienced, seen or heard about. We have tapes on breathing, dreaming, sneezing, living, and dying. We have emotional tapes of all kinds. No one has a tape exactly like ours and no one can completely understand any of our tapes.

Our computer can combine and run simultaneously many tapes. Our computer has the capability to self-destruct. Our computers all have the capability to multiply capacity beyond all the time and space. We have the capability to grow immediately into whatever the self decides. The self is the master of our computer. Our computer will do and be whatever the self dictates. It will do it automatically with searchings to discover all possible ways and put them into operation.

Chapter X—God

1. Ineffable

Our God created our Word. Our God is above and beyond, inside, outside, and indescribable. Our God is ineffable. Silence becomes a person in our God...and the violins of His trees and streams play music softly in His honor. Our God is love...and out and out and out into the unlimited space of our God through the myriad of silence and stars and the tremendous explosions of light and gas...our God flows and fills in His universe which He holds in the palm of His hand, as He stands in His heaven, which we cannot even dream of.

2. Treasures

"GIVE UP LITTLE THINGS FOR ME AND I WILL GIVE YOU BIGGER THINGS TO GIVE UP."...GOAL?...FREEDOM. "The truth will set you free: Whatever you give away you get to keep. The giving up is a storing up of treasure. Be ready to go so far as to lay down your life for a friend. Whatsoever you do the least you do to me. No other god before me – I am your only friend. I am in each and every person.

3. Call

Come with me outside, look at the night sky; see the stars, they go on forever. Come with me outside, into the warm sunlight, down to the ocean shore; see the waves. They shine at night, when the phosphorous lights them up. Come with me outside into the forest; see the trees and wild flowers. They came through the winter and into bloom from out of dirt and rocks. Come to me outside into the desert silence where small plants and grass grow. Silence is so good; it brings peace. Come to me outside of yourself, outside of your mind and into your heart; feel my love for you in all my creation. Come to me outside of this world into a new world of love and kindness, joy and goodness. I AM CALLING YOU, RIGHT NOW. I WANT YOU. You can be with me from now on.

      The choice is yours in each and every moment. See me in all that surrounds you for I am in the trees and the flowers and stars and the rocks, and in everything, but most of all I am in you and all living creatures, especially the people, each and every one that you see.

      I am the least. I am the poor. I am the sad. I am the cripple. I am the sick. I am the weak and the depressed. I took on all of these things out of my love for you. I took on your sins and your sicknesses and your diseases. I took the weight of them, so that you could be in my kingdom. My love for you has no limits. I love you as you are. I need your love. Can you choose to love me? I am the ones you despise. I am the ones you fear. I am the ones you reject. I am those you hate. I need your love, so that we can be together in my kingdom. My kingdom where only good will be. For my love has overcome the sins, the diseases, and the sicknesses of this world. They are burnt up in the fire of my love and gone forever.

4. Love Yourself

Tonight is full of stars and rocks and leaves....I come here not I but the spirit inside of me. Pray with me now that the flame of the spirit will burn bright and warm us all. Our God is practical. He makes things fit together; yet, His logic is beyond ours. He is in the opposite, mostly opposite from our thoughts of Him and others. He takes pain and creates kings with it. He takes manure and purifies flowers with it. He created each of us, none the same, each unique and therefore beautiful.

If I brought to you forty rocks none would be the same. If I brought to you all the rocks in and on the earth none would be the same.

If I brought to you forty leaves none would be the same. If I brought to you all the leaves from all the trees that ever grew not one leaf would be the same and this is true of blades of grass and grains of sand and stars in the sky.

If this is true for these things what about you? No one is the same as you. No one ever existed that was the same as you. You are unique and therefore beautiful. Did you know this? Can you take this in?...No! Not from me...But yes! You can take this into you. YOU CAN TELL YOURSELF each day and you will eventually start living. Unless you are conscious of your own beauty and value you are not really living because even when you share yourself with others it is a self that you do not value. So consider then what are you giving to the other person.

Here's how you can gain consciousness for your value. Go to a quiet place and listen to these words as you read them.

GOD DOES NOT MAKE JUNK. GOD MADE ME AS I AM. I AM REAL AND THEREFORE I MUST BE TRUE. MY HEART IS FULL OF LOVE FOR EVERYONE I MEET. IT IS ONLY NECESSARY FOR ME TO BE A FRIEND WHO LISTENS. I AM MY OWN BEST FRIEND BECAUSE I AM TRUE TO ME.

5. Desire to Love

To desire to love all, world and earth and all that's within….Do we compare collections of dinosaur bones with records of delinquents and criminals? We are rocks in the river of life tumbled by the living water. The love in the masses, in the crowds, caught everyone on fire with joy. Smiles lit the faces of all, so that happiness grew throughout the area and stretched out to cover the land. As we stood there time had no meaning. The joy was so great, eternity upon eternity flew by and still we were there in love.

The world is changing rapidly. South America is going through a tremendous upheaval. The Middle East is like a bomb. Earthquakes occur regularly along with floods and changing weather patterns. The spirit of the Lord is crying out for a lasting residence in the heart of mankind. We must become more open to the spirit of Jesus. It is not easy to commit to it, to the "I love you" to each in each moment. Be comforted; the spirit within you is the source of all power.

6. Special

      I want you to know you are special. I want you to know you are beautiful. These things I write I am saying to you alone, right to your heart. There is no other you! There never was and never will be anyone like you. So! You are special! And, you are beautiful and powerful! Each BREATH YOU TAKE MAKES YOU BRAND NEW. Listen! Hear! These words are true. Decide to renew your feelings for forgiving others. Decide to get into really caring for other people. Throw out pity and bring in truth.

7. Today's Life

      The facts of life, all there is to know about the birds and the bees, sex education and biological urges, etc., etc., etc., kids need to know?...Yes, but the truth and in perspective. Please dear people do not leave it up to J.R. or TV and do not leave out family, and family is a necessity in the normal development of a child. We live in a world of not enough Dads at home. We live in world where reality takes the back seat to the unreal—where milk comes from bottles and plastic or paper containers...a crazy world where the burning of dead rotten bodies has become the fuel for our transportation, and many people smoke dried leaves covered with dried fly manure to show how macho they are. Our women and even some of our men pour urine (perfume's base ingredient) on themselves so that they will smell just right. We use the intestinal scrapings of animals for makeup so that our ladies will look pretty. How we look has become more important than how we feel and think. In order to bring out some of the real facts of life and living I offer to all of you these mostly short writings. They are the thoughts that have come through me to you from the source within. Remember the core of all of us is good. Life is a lesson in love. We are all teachers by example. We are the responsibility of each other. We are the cause of all of our own disasters. Until we recognize our oneness and recognize the source of our good and our safety, we are lost.

Life holds unlimited patterns because we are all individual selves. He awaits our acknowledgement of His unlimited and eternal love. His love is unceasing. In life, we sometimes experience ridicule when we are not at fault, or we experience praise when we did nothing to deserve it. And, we decide which is the better place: to have cheated and won or to have lost and been true? Which is the better place?

8. To Grow

Every crippled, sick child, every drugged and dirty child, and every foreign child is important beyond all measure. At the moment we consider ourselves better, more important, or more powerful, at that moment we become less and we cease to grow....

9. Thoughts

What you think of yourself is what you get back from other people. What you pass out you get to keep. So if you are not satisfied with what you are getting from others you must change your own self-image because you are the source for you. There is a simple way to solve this concern about self and that is to get out of yourself and put God in the place of self. Not that you are God but that God becomes the controller of you. Remember He is the real source.

10. To Love Anyone

Sirens screaming. Music blaring. Cars, trucks, and motorcycles racing. So very busy, so very loud, not aware of the wind and the trees and the flowers, and dead to the reality and the flow of life, the city cries out for peace amid the confusion and the sicknesses of its young and its' old. Let's get together; let's love one another right now Love is not a physical thing. It has no beginning and no ending. "To love anyone is to hope in him for always. The moment we judge anyone and reduce him to what we know of him, he ceases to be able to become better. We must expect everything of everyone. We must dare to be love in a world that does not know love." (Charles de Foucauld) If you are conscious of the things in your life that need changing then reach out for help, share your troubles and your problems with people who can help you get free. Go off like Dorothy in the Wizard of Oz, leaving the things that pull you down, and change the direction of your life. No one else can push the buttons on your computer. Know for sure that you are loved.

11. Love Is One

Love is not separate, it is one. It is like making the water level. Only the damned hold back the waters of love. Tears are the waters that surround the embryo of the soul.

12. Lord

Direct me, us, help us to be for you and with you in each moment of our days. Help us to be sure of our goodness and to trust in kindness, its power and value. Help us to be listening for your voice coming from places least likely. Direct us in the little as well as the big things.

Our lives are like a variety of packages of good things: present, food, clothing, fresh water and more. As we live we have the exclusive right to give these gifts away to whomever we choose or to hold them back. Add to this the interesting thought that there is a special path made for each of us. A path that will allow us to meet the special ones these packages were meant for. Lord, you know the problem the world is in. You see the people not realizing the specialness of themselves, or the gifts, and not willing to wait for the right path to open. Direct us Lord, Help us...

13. Life and Death

We are all in an eternal mode, the life here in the world is transitory. We have been told to set the eyes of our heart on heaven, not on this world. "My kingdom is not of this world." We are not to be concerned with the mistakes of others, we are to forgive them and know that Jesus will be the judge of our loving or not loving.

We are like faucets. Fresh water flows from a fresh water faucet. Sewage flows from a faucet connected to the sewer. A faucet on the sewer will never flow fresh water and a faucet on a fresh water system will never flow sewage.

Jesus came to bring peace, a peace the world cannot give. He did not come to bring war, he did not fight back, and he forgave the men as they nailed him to the cross. All war is sewage.

A priest is supposed to be a source of food to the people, a source of living water, and source of hope in the world. If a priest is going around spreading the news that war is a necessary thing and that evil is winning and will take over the world, and if this and if that, he leaves those people without hope; for the faucet of a priest needs to be flowing with only hope and love and food and living water.

Jesus came to bring life, He did not carry a weapon. We have His spirit for our protection and consolation. You can write me off and say I have never experienced real poverty; but, that would not be quite true because I have known another kind of poverty – the poverty of spirit. I have tried to do it all myself and found that it leads to war. Unless we have the spirit the martyrs had, we will not be happy with ourselves or with the results of our lives. The Crusades were antichrist. They did not fit with, "Love your enemies, do good to those that hurt you." We are in an eternal mode, whatever we give out we get to keep. If we give out war we get to keep war.

14. Grace

The Grace (love) of God holds us all together and fits the little things into place. When things break down and money is short and sickness comes on, be happy because Grace will soon flow in to fill and smooth and to bring peace, gentle peace. Forgive and Grace will fill your heart's void. Decide to love, step over the edge. Say Yes to God....

15. More

Always more—Not enough—Different but not enough—more. The world has no solution. The stars go on forever. But forever is just more and more stars. Only one person is the answer to more. He alone is enough. With Him everything makes sense. Without Him nothing is. Every time a person seeks for more he is alone. Is that more? All other paths are futile, a waste. Jesus Christ is Lord. He is the Lord of all abundance. The desire of our heart is only fulfilled in Him. He is the enough and the more. He is the beginning and the end of all searching. When we lose Him or do not find Him we lose love and the ability to love. He is love, there is no other. He established a church in the world. His church has all His teachings set out in a clear and simple way. We love His church. Those who attack it we also love. Be they enemies, brothers, sons, daughters, priest, nuns or others, His love has conquered death. His love will shine forth from His church forever. There is in the will of God no other church and the will of the Father will be. Arguments are useless. What is...IS! What will be only God knows. So He tells us to love, not only our friends, but all people including our enemies. Especially our enemies. If we in the moments follow Him. We have WHAT IS!

16. The Presence

We have been given much if we are conscious of His presence. The decision is to love. It is each person's decision in each moment of life. Once we decide to love, the world changes and the sun shines into the dark corners of our minds and the broom of forgiveness sweeps through us. Forgiveness enhances acceptance, and love flows and is allowed to wash away the garbage.

Through His example, we shall know Him, and the sun still brightens the land, and charity gives it a hand. You can live a life of love. If you want to you can. He is present in us and in each and every one we meet.

17. Man's Highest Activity

God creates and man...? Yes, man creates, too. For from the Father to the Son passes the will to restore and make new. So the highest activity of man is to create. God is the material; God is the supply; God is the energy; and God is the power. God inspires and man desires.

Life holds unlimited patterns. The flowing lines become woven into our things. Patterns God has given so that we may have creations pleasing to us and to Him.

In our creations we honor God even when our intentions are otherwise. Let it be! Let it be! Let it be!

Mary had a little Lamb whose fleece was white as snow, and everywhere that Mary went the Lamb was sure to go. It followed her to school one day which was against the rules. It made the children laugh and play to see a Lamb at school

18. The Heart

Love has no car; love has no clothes; love has no ballgames; love has no fancy food; love has no television; love has only you and me; love needs no physical body; love needs no earthen world; love needs no starry sky; love needs no far off galaxies; and love needs no unlimited universe. Love needs only human hearts. The heart is not the physical par; it is where the kingdom is—on the other side—in the opposite—beyond the mirror. Our eyes see reflection; our hearts see reality.

In the opposite, what seems tragedy becomes treasure and what is pain becomes pure gold. We have examples: manure becomes fertilizer and brings forth flowers, the exploding of gasoline becomes transportation. The leaves that fall become food for the small trees. In the opposite, death becomes resurrection.

19. On Being—On Going

Where your heart is, that is where you are. Through daily living we must honor God and do His work. Let's see, when we go to a ballgame, are we doing the work of Christ? He said, "Put aside the things of children." When we play golf, or join the army or navy, are we doing

Christ's work? He said, "Love your enemy; do good to those who hurt you." When we eat gourmet food, are we doing Christ's work? "Don't consider the food you eat." When we gossip, are we doing Christ's work? He said look at your own faults before you fault others. When we go to Las Vegas, are we doing Christ's work? He said: Feed my lambs, feed my sheep:...slot machines?...When we drive a car, the fumes are poisonous. When we watch television...lonely people cry out for visits and conversation. Fear closes in and boxes up. In our schools do we do Christ's work? "Go and teach all the nations"....but in school...? When we walk along the street, passing people, do we smile and say, "hello"? "Whatsoever you do to the least of these, you do it unto me." When we dress up with lots of makeup?... "The humble shall be in the kingdom." The kingdom is of the heart not of this world.

20. Together

When the day is done, when the car is cold, when supper is through, when the last dish is done and safe on the cupboard shelf, when the TV is off and the doors are locked for the night, when the children are tucked in and finally asleep, when we find ourselves alone and together in the quiet, it is then we must take the time to say to each other all the things that will put us back together and keep us strong and alive. For, together, we can meet and overcome the afflictions of the world.

To grow we need to go deep inside. Deep in our heart of hearts we must hold a place for everyone. It is a place of glowing warmth, a place of kindness and caring. Each other one is there without effort, there, yet free. And our hope is that each of you will hold a place deep inside of your hearts for us. Love is mysterious. I love you all.

P.S. The way to grow the most is to forgive and hold a place for our enemies in our hearts. We must expand to this. Happiness is a mystery, not a goal.

21. Now is the Time

Into where, from nowhere, and yet we were there, but unaware; so we did not care. Why are you and I alive?...to learn to drive?...to learn to strive? or to just arrive?...hopeless?...no!...helpless?...yes! But though I think I am helpless, I am not. For God is with me. We, you and I, all of us are alive to the extent we live in the hearts of those who love us. We are alive to the extent that we love. If I am loved, I cannot die. If I love, the one I love lives forever, for we keep our loved ones deep in our hearts, safe, clean, warm and whole. We restore them. We make them new.

Now is the moment
Now is the time
Day is too long
To be is the goal
The growth of a soul
Time holds the key

To love makes you free
So take it by fives
And take deeper dives
Because love never dies

      A mystery it is as each five minutes roll by – ineffable, infinitely perfect, infinitely alive, enwrapped and enfolded in love, like a rose. How do I judge? By not listening to you, by not sharing with you. The bird is free at last. He made the decision. He made the changes possible and the changes happened. The bird!...Yes! the bird is free at last.

Birds don't work?
Birds don't pay rent?
Birds don't lie and cheat?
Birds don't steal?
Birds don't horde all the grain?
Birds are smart enough not to go out in the rain?
Some birds that is!

22. Civilization

      We take dead stars to make our cars. We take dead and rotten bodies to make our fuel. We tear out flowers and we mix dead rotten bodies and dead stars to make our roads. We drink the juice of rotten plants and smoke dried leaves covered with fly manure while we drive on the dead mix, burning the dead and rotten body fuel, to a ballgame we should have stopped playing when we were babies.

While we drive we pass through cemented streets, past steel reinforced buildings void of trees, flowers and plants, and through neighborhoods filled with the rotten body smoke that eats away at our lungs and makes us cough and burns our eyes. When we get to the ballgame we enter the stadium where the seats and the steps are covered with paper wrappings and cups that covered poison and we in turn go and buy poison in cups and paper wrappings. As we eat and drink the poison and through the wrappers we yell and curse at the players. Then we all jam to get out of the stadium and curse and scream and yell at the other drivers as we again pass through the scenes of death and futility on our way home. Home a box-like structure with a toilet attached much like a cage in some filthy zoo. And unless we have found the door to heartland this is what we call living.
OR

We go to what we call work, shuffling and stamping pieces of paper that transfer, store and cash other pieces of paper and we store paper in boxes and call people and tell them numbers that they write on other pieces of papers and make prints of pieces of paper and make copies of the prints and revise and stamp and store, etc.... Then we go home and as we go toward home we sometimes realize but most often not that the most valuable paper used during the day was in the toilet.
OR

We plant seeds in neat tractor made rows and when the plants are little we spray them with poison to kill the hundreds and thousands of bugs that come to attack them. Then as they grow we spray them again and again and actually poison them in the process never quite killing all the bugs, that, if we had been smart, we would have eaten in the first place.

23. Follow

Come follow me amid the flurry and the violence of life today. Come follow me as nations stand defying the very existence of our Father. Come follow me as your brothers and sisters ignore and betray and talk against my church. Come follow me in times of pain and sorrow. Come follow me through the loneliness of the cross….Life is not easy. The struggle to learn and the struggle to realize truth in the world is very difficult unless you give over to me each moment. Let me be the presence within you. Humble yourself so that I can be that patience you need.

Read again and again the book that I have left for you, so full of examples of the people before you who struggled with each and every one of the problems you now face.

He walks along and the trail of His footsteps leaves a path for those who follow along the way.

24. His Plan

Jesus, you are the teacher in us all. We thank You and we praise You that Your will is done in our lives in spite of ourselves. Thank you, Lord, for drawing us to You. You are truly the Lamb of God. "If I be lifted up upon the cross, I will draw everyone to me." He will draw to himself you and me and everyone. And as we grow we have thoughts of the magnitude and the extent of this drawing. We cannot imagine or contain these thoughts. We cannot think UNLIMITED or ETERNAL, yet NOW contains it—now and now and now. Wow!

25. Seasoning

The seasons: Spring, Summer, Fall, and Winter. Spring is like finding faith, fresh, delicate, clean and clear. What follows is the Summer of God's warm love. Then we Fall and love seems far away, and the world is cold, Winter. In living, we see the pattern. And finding these are but symbols for man so that he can choose eternal Spring and Summer.

26. The Passageway

The passing, the passage, life is a passageway. The true man knows the way, Jesus! The loving God is unlimited and eternal. He wants man to choose to love Him. Love is not a physical thing, or idea or person. Love transcends the world. Love overcomes the world. Love will eventually melt the world and make it less than necessary.

27. Se man Tics

The fact is, we are covered with bugs; but ticks are by far the worst bug, for they burrow into you and suck blood and grow fat. They separate your life from you and put it in little bags which are their bodies. Words can do this, too. Like ticks, words can hold your life blood. Screw them out of you, one at a time. Turn slowly, counter-clockwise; only accept into you words that flow openly in and out. Take into you the rich flow from the hearts of those who truly love. Get rid of the ticks which weaken you with their repeated sucking.

Words are the most dangerous tools; words are the most dangerous of poisons. Words are the most explosive elements; words are the most flammable fuel. And, words can also be the opposite of all these. Words hold the world together. Words spark the energy that holds the stars. Words can lift you up beyond your body, beyond the earth and millions of light years into space to places and wonders and joy unbelievable. Words are!

www.ingramcontent.com/pod-product-compliance
Lightning Source LLC
Chambersburg PA
CBHW020012050426
42450CB00005B/428